THE LIFE CYCLE OF A

FROG

By Robin Merritt

Published by The Child's World®
1980 Lookout Drive
Mankato, MN 56003-1705
800-599-READ
www.childsworld.com

The Child's World®: Mary Berendes, Publishing Director
The Design Lab: Kathleen Petelinsek, design
Red Line Editorial: Editorial direction

Photographs ©: Carmen Martínez Banús/iStockphoto, cover
(top left, bottom right), 1 (top left, bottom right), 3; Debbie
Oetgen/Shutterstock Images, cover (top right, bottom left), 1
(top right, bottom left), 31 (top); Sascha Burkard/Fotolia, 5;
Mark Grenier/Shutterstock Images, 6; Cathy Keifer/Shutterstock
Images, 9; Joshua Haviv/Shutterstock Images, 10; iStockphoto,
13, 25, 26; Hans Pfletschinger/Photolibrary, 14, 17, 30 (top,
bottom); Matt Hart/Shutterstock Images, 18; Cynthia Kidwell/
Shutterstock Images, 21, 31 (bottom); Shutterstock Images, 22;
Andrew Howe/iStockphoto, 29

Copyright © 2012 by The Child's World®

ISBN: 978-1-60973-150-2
LCCN: 2011927738

Printed in the United States of America
Mankato, MN
July 2011
PA02089

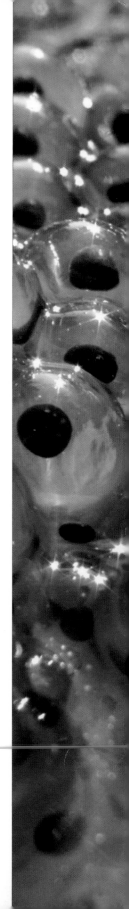

T A B L E O F
CONTENTS

LIFE CYCLES

Every living thing has a life cycle. A life cycle is the steps a living thing goes through as it grows and changes. Humans have a life cycle. Animals have a life cycle. Plants have a life cycle, too.

A cycle is something that happens over and over again. A life cycle begins with the start of a new life. It continues as a plant or creature grows. And it keeps going as one living thing creates another, or **reproduces**—and the cycle starts over again.

A frog's life cycle has four main steps: egg, **tadpole**, froglet, and adult frog.

Both frogs and plants have life cycles.

Adult frogs breathe air like people do.

FROGS

Frogs are **amphibians**. Like salamanders and toads, frogs live part of their lives in water and part on land. Adult frogs can stay out of the water at least some of the time. But baby frogs, or tadpoles, must always live in the water. Tadpoles have **gills** to breathe in the water like fish. Adult frogs have lungs they use to breathe like people do. But they can also breathe through their skin.

An adult frog has a round body with no tail. Its back legs are longer than its front legs. This helps it jump very high. A frog has webbed feet to help it swim. It has big, bulging eyes that can look around for food and enemies. It uses its long, sticky tongue to catch its meals.

Many frogs may live around ponds, lakes, streams, or marshes. Some also live in rain forests. Because they need to keep their skin wet, frogs like wet or damp places. Even dew on the grass helps their skin stay moist.

A frog's sticky tongue catches flies and other insects.

A frog warms its body in the sun.

Like other amphibians, frogs are cold-blooded. This means a frog's body temperature changes depending on where it is sitting. If a frog is in a cold lake, its body temperature falls. If it is sitting in the hot sun, its body temperature rises.

There are more than 5,000 kinds of frogs. They live everywhere in the world except Antarctica. Some are tiny, like the hip-pocket frog, which is no bigger than a thumbnail. But a goliath frog may weigh as much as a pet cat.

Some frogs have patterns on their skin. They blend into their surroundings. They can hide from predators and stalk prey without being seen. The skin of leaf frogs has ridges like leaf veins. It matches the color of dead leaves. There are very colorful frogs, too. They are usually poisonous.

Some tiny frogs can fit on a person's fingertip.

A frog **embryo** grows inside its egg.

HATCHING

A female frog lays its eggs in water or on grass or leaves. Each egg is inside a clear ball of jelly. The many eggs clump together. The jelly protects the eggs from hungry fish or other creatures. Inside each egg, a tiny frog embryo grows. It gets the nutrients it needs to grow from the egg's yolk. As it gets bigger, it wiggles inside the jelly covering.

After a few days, the baby frog escapes from the protective jelly. Now it is a tadpole. It looks like a little fish with a big head and long tail.

TADPOLE

Like a fish, a tadpole has gills. When water flows over the gills, a tadpole takes oxygen from the water to breathe.

A tadpole cannot swim right after hatching. It needs to rest first. It clings to an underwater plant and keeps feeding off the last of its egg yolk, which is in its body. After a few days, the tadpole flicks its tail and swims off.

Tadpoles breathe with gills.

Four legs grow from bumps on a tadpole's body.

GROWING AND CHANGING

A tadpole spends most of its time eating. It eats lots of **algae**, which are tiny water plants. Most tadpoles are **herbivores**, animals that eat plants instead of animals.

A tadpole eats and grows, eats and grows. It swims and hides, too. It must escape turtles, fish, or other hungry animals that try to eat it.

Soon, two tiny bumps grow at the base of its tail. These little bumps keep growing and become back legs. After the tadpole's back legs start growing, its front legs grow, too. It can still swim well with the help of four webbed feet.

The tadpole's body changes inside, too. As a tadpole grows, it develops lungs, which help it breathe on land. Skin grows over the tadpole's gills and they disappear. Soon it must swim to the water surface to get a breath of air.

When a tadpole has front and back legs and its lungs have developed, it is ready to climb out of the water and onto land. It still has a tail and is smaller than an adult, so it is called a froglet. Soon the tail will shrink until it disappears.

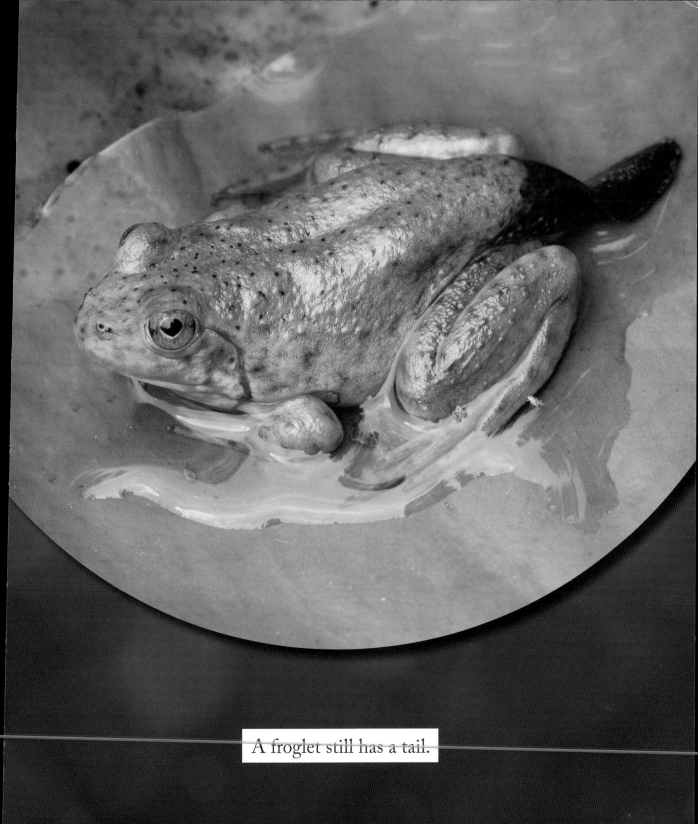

A froglet still has a tail.

A strawberry poison dart frog becomes an adult quickly.

AN ADULT FROG

Depending on the species, a frog becomes an adult months to years after it hatches. A strawberry poison dart frog becomes an adult in just three weeks. But a bullfrog can take more than a year. The set of changes a frog goes through to become an adult is called its **metamorphosis**.

Frogs can live anywhere from four to 25 years. To live long, they must keep away from predators. To escape a raccoon on the shore, a frog leaps into the water. To escape a snapping turtle in the pond, the frog jumps onto a floating log.

Unlike tadpoles, adult frogs are **carnivores**. They eat other animals. A frog watches and waits for a fly. Its long sticky tongue flashes out and snatches the fly. The frog's large eyeballs push down onto its mouth, helping it swallow. Frogs eat beetles, worms, slugs, small snakes, and even other frogs.

Food becomes harder to find in the winter. **Hibernating** frogs escape hunger and cold weather. A leopard frog swims to the bottom of a pond. Its heartbeat slows and it breathes through its skin. In spring, it swims to the surface again.

Frogs eat worms and other animals.

A male marsh frog inflates two sacs on its body to sing its song.

FINDING A MATE

Many frogs mate in early spring. Male and female frogs come together to create new frogs. When leopard frogs are ready to mate, the males gather at a pond and call to attract females. The call of a leopard frog sounds like a low snore, but each species sounds different. At last female frogs arrive. Some species of female frogs choose a male frog with the deepest and loudest voice. In other species, the females choose males with the most complex songs.

LAYING EGGS

A female frog lays hundreds or thousands of eggs in the water, and the male frog **fertilizes** them. The female leopard frog leaves the pond, but the male will stay and try to mate with other females. Some species care for their eggs and tadpoles, but others do not care for their young. Some eggs will not survive. Fish and other animals eat the eggs. After seven to ten days, a tadpole hatches from one of the eggs. The frog life cycle continues.

After a frog lays its eggs, new tadpoles hatch.

LIFE CYCLE DIAGRAM

Egg

Tadpole

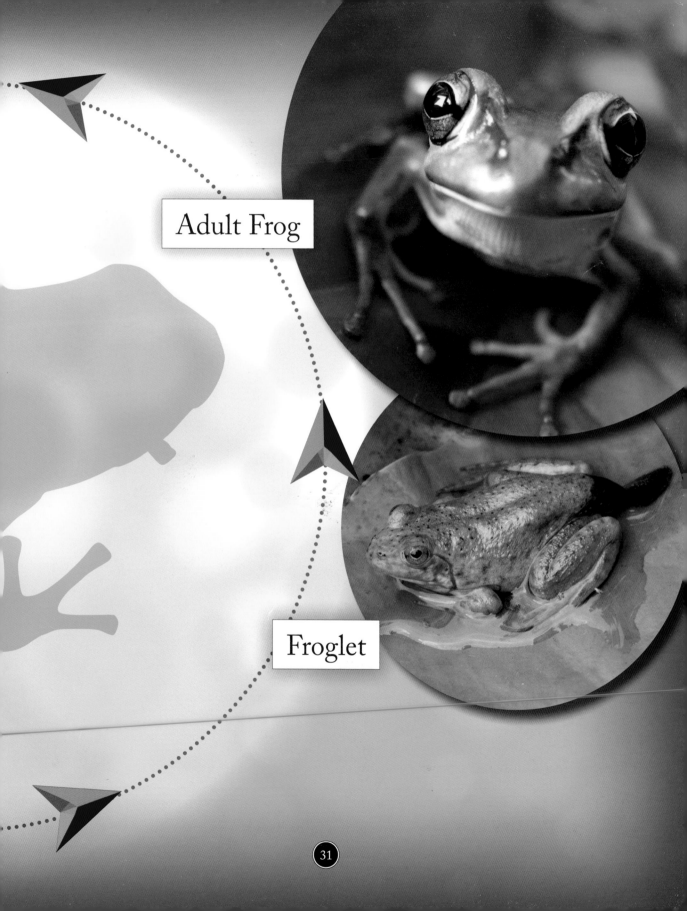

Adult Frog

Froglet

Web Sites

Visit our Web site for links about the life cycle of a frog:
childsworld.com/links

Note to Parents, Teachers, and Librarians: We routinely verify our Web links to make sure they are safe and active sites. So encourage your readers to check them out!

Glossary

algae (AL-jee): Algae are tiny plants that have no leaves or stems and that grow in water. Tadpoles eat algae.

amphibians (am-FIB-ee-uns): Amphibians are animals that live part of their lives in the water and part on land. Frogs are amphibians.

carnivores (CAR-nuh-vors): Carnivores are animals that eat other animals. Adult frogs are carnivores.

embryo (EM-bree-oh): An embryo is an organism in the early stages of growth. A frog embryo grows in its egg.

fertilizes (FUR-tuh-ly-zez): When a male cell fertilizes a female cell, it becomes able to grow and develop into a new life. A male frog fertilizes eggs laid by a female frog.

gills (GILS): Gills are the body part that a tadpole or fish uses to take air from water to breathe. Tadpoles use their gills to breathe.

herbivores (HUR-buh-vors): Herbivores are animals that eat plants, not other animals. Most tadpoles are herbivores.

hibernating (HYE-bur-nate-ing): Hibernating animals and insects spend winters in a deep sleep, with slowed breathing and heartbeat. Some frogs spend winters hibernating.

metamorphosis (met-uh-MOR-fuh-siss): Metamorphosis is the series of changes some animals go through between hatching and adulthood. A tadpole is one part of a frog's metamorphosis.

reproduces (ree-pruh-DOOS-ez): If an animal or plant reproduces, it produces offspring. A frog reproduces when it has baby frogs.

tadpole (TAD-pole): A tadpole is a baby frog that lives in the water. A tadpole grows to become an adult frog.

Books

Bailer, Darice. *How Do Tadpoles Become Frogs?* New York: Marshall Cavendish Benchmark, 2011.

Bekkering, Annalise. *Frogs.* New York: Weigl, 2011.

Clarke, Barry. *Amphibian (Eyewitness Books).* New York Dorling Kindersley, 2005.

Kingston, Anna. *The Life Cycle of a Poison Dart Frog (Nature's Life Cycles).* New York: Gareth Stevens Publishing, 2011.

Stewart, Melissa. *A Place for Frogs.* Atlanta, GA: Peachtree. 2009.

Index